LET'S GET MONSTER SMASHED

HORROR MOVIE DRINKS FOR A **KILLER** TIME

LET'S GET MONSTER SMASHED

HORROR MOVIE DRINKS FOR A KILLER TIME

JON CHAIET & MARC CHAIET

4880 Lower Valley Road • Atglen, PA 19310

There are many influences that played a part in the creation of this book. Many people who facilitated its culmination, old and new. Many people to thank and recognize with gratitude.

So I'd like to dedicate this book to you, the person reading this. Without you, none of this would be possible.

MARC

For Missa, forever.

JON

CONTENTS

GREETINGS! 7
SPIRITS & INGREDIENTS 8
TOOLS OF THE TRADE 12
TECHNIQUES & TACTICS 15
SATANIC SYRUPS 17
PUPPET MASTER PICK 19

MONSTER SHOTS 21
TASTY TRAVESTIES OF SCIENCE AND NATURE!

GELATINOUS GULPS 53
MUTANT GOO FROM ANOTHER GALAXY!

POTIONS & GROG 75
WITCHES BREW IN CAULDRON-SIZED PORTIONS!

SMOKE & MIRRORS 97
SPECIAL FX TO ASTOUND AND ENDRUNKEN!

VIRGIN SACRIFICES 119
EVERY GOOD PARTY NEEDS A SACRIFICIAL LAMB

INDEX 140

WELCOME TO *LET'S GET MONSTER SMASHED*! DELICIOUS, DEVIANT DRINKS TO DOWN WHILE YOU AND FRIENDS FEAST ON ALL OF YOUR FAVORITE FRIGHTFUL FLICKS.

Like many small town New Jersey kids raised with little adult supervision, we grew up early on the classic camp and visceral violence of horror movies from the '80s and '90s. Also like many from Jersey, we've developed a deep love for booze and its plethora of palette-pleasing potables.

Witness *Let's Get Monster Smashed*, the deformed mutant baby of that unholy union! Like our favorite movies, the recipes here are a mix of vintage favorites and new classics—weirdly wonderful and unexpectedly unique. Whether the party demons demand shots, punches, or something with a little more sorcery, you'll find it all within this twisted tome.

So join us now on a journey through hellish dimensions (or maybe just to your kitchen and then back to the couch) as we construct a collection of cocktails so curious and captivating that you and your crowd will be clamoring for more!

JON & MARC

SPIRITS & INGREDIENTS

AN ALCOHOL LIST AS DEMONICALLY DIVERSE AND WACKILY WEIRD AS YOUR MOST-LOVED MOVIES! THE SOURCE MATERIAL MAY BE LOW-BROW, BUT GREAT DRINKS ALL START WITH GREAT INGREDIENTS.

Herein lies a breadth of booze and broth so broad, fear not if you don't recognize something. The dark gods aren't especially fastidious about which label of liquor you use, but there are a few fixins within this toxic tome where substitutions just aren't suitable.

But listen closely, dear reader: You needn't purchase all these palliatives to enjoy this eerie encyclopedia. Friends, film, and festivities should always be at the forefront. And you could always just *steal* the booze.

GIN: A spirit contrived from the distillation of fermented grain mash and fiercely flavored with juniper and other botanicals. The shadow spirits also demand Sloe Gin, which is sweeter and fruit-flavored.

RUM: A spirit coerced from the bizarre byproducts of sugarcane processing—like molasses—or from the fresh-pressed juice of the sugar cane. Rums range from white and light to golden and dark or spiced. Our truculent trifecta includes a dark, a white, and a high-proof 151 white.

TEQUILA: A spirit created from the dreaded distillation of the roasted and fermented blue agave plant, which is then aged in wooden casks.

WHISKEY: The dark king. A spirit conjured from the devilish distillation of fermented grain mash, which is then aged in wooden casks (or not, if you like moonshine or white dog whiskey). Irish, Canadian, Japanese; honey or cinnamon-flavored, with the "e" or without, it really doesn't matter—we generally only care about American bourbon. Sweet, delicious, American bourbon.

MEZCAL: Tequila's smoky spectre. A distilled spirit cooked up from the manic maguey plant, which is roasted in the ground and then fermented.

BRANDY: A spirit constructed from the distillation of wine, often available in fanciful flavors.

COGNAC: A frighteningly French brandy which must be crafted according to very strict standards of grapes, distillation, and maturation.

VODKA: A frequently flavorless spirit crafted from the distillation of fermented grains, potatoes, fruits, or sugars. The rich recipes ahead demand dreadful deviations; marshmallow, cotton candy, popcorn, and a black variety.

APPLEJACK: The original and oldest American spirit; an apple brandy that originated in New Jersey, just like the Toxic Avenger.

ABSINTHE: An anise-flavored spirit concocted with herbs and botanicals, most notoriously the wicked wormwood.

BÉNÉDICTINE: An aromatic brandy-based liqueur with a (possibly haunted) secret recipe.

CHAMPAGNE: A French sparkling white wine.

MALBEC: A red wine with full flavors of fruit and chocolate.

SAKE: A Japanese rice wine created by fermenting polished rice that's then brewed similarly to beer.

BEER: A carbonated alcoholic beverage crafted from the brewing of malted barley and flavored with hops.

GINGER BEER: A sweet, creepily carbonated non-alcoholic beverage made from the fermentation of ginger, yeast, and sugar.

CHARTREUSE: A French liqueur made by Carthusian monks since the 1730s from a recipe of over 130 flowers, herbs, and plants. So good they named a fuckin' color after it.

FERNET-BRANCA: An amaro, or bitter herbal liqueur. Suspiciously strong and antiseptic in flavor—great for the gut.

CHERRY HEERING: A sickly sweet cherry Danish liqueur.

LILLET BLANC: A French aperitif produced from an aromatic wine flavored with citrus.

COINTREAU: A brand of triple sec, an orange-flavored liqueur.

WALNUT LIQUEUR: A sweet, nut-flavored liqueur with low alcohol content.

LICOR 43 (CUARENTA Y TRES): Your dad probably loves this sweet Spanish liqueur derived from citrus & fruit, and flavored with vanilla and other herbs & spices.

COFFEE LIQUEUR:
A liqueur typically made from a grain-neutral spirit infused with coffee and other flavors.

CREAM LIQUEUR:
A liqueur made from Irish whiskey and cream (informative, we know).

CHOCOLATE LIQUEUR:
Also known as creme de cacao, this chocolate-flavored liqueur can also have hints of coconut, orange, or vanilla.

CREME DE CASSIS:
A sweet, dark liqueur made from black currants.

MIDORI MELON LIQUEUR:
A sweet, muskmelon-flavored liqueur with a grossly green color.

BLUE CURAÇAO:
A bright blue citrus-flavored liqueur made from dried citrus peels and spices. And E133 Brilliant Blue—lots of E133 Brilliant Blue.

99 BANANAS:
A sickeningly sweet banana-flavored liqueur.

ANGOSTURA BITTERS:
A concentrated bitter herbal tincture used to flavor drinks by the drop.

PEYCHAUD'S BITTERS:
A gentian-based bitter with hints of anise and cherry.

ORANGE FLOWER WATER:
An essential water distilled from fresh bitter orange blossoms.

ENERGY DRINKS:
Super sweet and swelling with stimulants, this swill comes in various flavors and colors. But be sure to use a beverage containing B vitamins; only these will allow it to glow under blacklight.

FRUIT & VEGETABLE JUICES:
It's like the blood of plants! The fresher the better.

MATCHA:
A finely-ground powder of specially grown green tea.

SOY LECITHIN:
A food additive with a variety of uses; we add it to liquids as an emulsifying agent to create a foam.

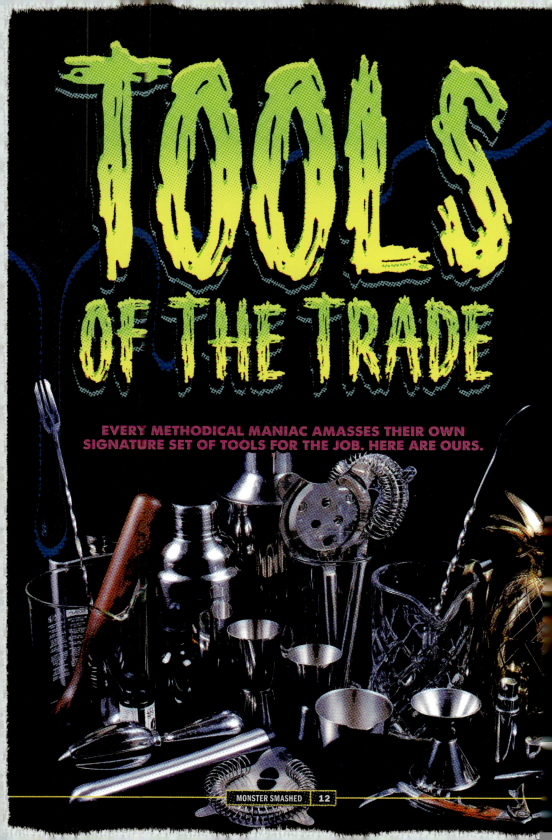

JIGGER: A demonic dual-cupped measuring device with standard volumes used to quickly measure out liquid ingredients.

MEASURING CUPS: Satanic staggered-sized cups used to measure dry ingredients. If you're having trouble converting liquid ounces to cups, standard liquid measuring cups typically display ounces alongside the standard measurements. Don't forget, kids! 1 cup equals 8 ounces.

MIXING GLASS: A (usually very fancy) glass used only for stirring purely spirits-based cocktails with ice.

COCKTAIL SHAKER: Two choices await thee: The devilish 2-cup Boston version or the strainer-included Cobbler variety. The same technique is used on both: Add ice and booze, and then shake the shit out of it. Don't forget to strain!

COCKTAIL STRAINER: Again, there are 2 vile varieties: The Hawthorne and the Julep. If you have a Cobbler shaker with a built-in strainer you may not even need one. (You need one, trust us.)

STIRRING SPOON: A loathsome long-stemmed spoon for mixing cocktails with a twisted stem for fast stirring and occasionally a pitchfork end.

NOVELTY GLASSES: A frighteningly phenomenal cocktail is all about the absolute freshest ingredients being conjured in masterful ways to excite and enliven, and the vessel should follow suit. But sometimes a grossly great drink just needs to be served in a novelty toilet bowl-shaped shot glass.

BUNDT CAKE PAN: Just like grandma used to beat us with!

PETRI DISHES: Used in this wicked work to make individual jello shots, so make sure they're not too large.

SYRINGES: A large food-safe syringe for dosing out bulbous batches into cramped cauldrons and smaller ones for individual syringe shots. Needles optional.

KNIFE: No matter the immensity of your instrument, a razor's edge is expedient. You never know when a psycho killer will show up at your bar.

BLENDER: Sundry spinning blades that mince, mangle, and mix. Watch those fingers!

HAND BLENDER: A humble hand-held stick blender used to integrate air directly.

COOKIE SHEET: Transferring teeming tubs of germinating gelatin to a chilly ice chest is a tiny task with hefty hardware. Get one with edges (so yes, technically a jellyroll pan. Nerd.)

POT: No, not *that* kind (well, not *only* that kind), the kind you cook things in!

WAX PAPER: Cooking paper imbued with wax to make it water and grease-proof.

CHEESECLOTH: A lank, loosely-woven cotton cloth for straining out puny particulates.

CULINARY TORCH: A bantam blow torch that uses food-grade propane for pinpoint hellfire.

PLASTIC MASK: A strange request from the party gods, but one we must fulfill nonetheless. Guarantee it's generic, without face holes.

RUBBER GLOVES: Little latex gloves. Wash them out!

BLACKLIGHT: A smattering of swigs sparkle and splendor under UV light. Prepare the party zone painstakingly.

MASON JAR: A ghastly glass jar with tight-fitting lid for infusing or canning ingredients.

GLASSWARE

A plethora of potables requires a variety of vessels. Here's what we'll use for the reprobate recipes ahead:

SHOT GLASS

ROCKS GLASS

PUNCH GLASS

HIGHBALL GLASS

PINT GLASS

TECHNIQUES & TACTICS

MASTER THE DARK ARTS OF DRINK-MAKING BY STUDYING EACH OF THESE TABOO TECHNIQUES IN A TREK TOWARD INEFFABLE INEBRIATION.

FLAVOR INFUSIONS: Furnishing flavor from a solid ingredient to a liquid is as uncomplicated as letting the lot steep for a day or two.

RIMMING: Moisten the rim of a glass (usually using a lemon or lime wedge) and then gently press it into the dry ingredient, which has been spread evenly on to a small plate.

SHAKE WITH ICE AND STRAIN: Combine the loathsome liquid ingredients into a cocktail shaker with ice, seal the lid or second cup tightly, then shake the soul out of that sucker for at least 10 seconds. Bring the shaker up horizontally over your shoulder while shaking for maximum mixing

LAYERING: Crafting a layered cocktail, or pousse-café, takes forbearance, finesse, and fortune. Build the beverage (heavy liquids first) by slowly pouring each ingredient over the belly of an upturned spoon held just above the glass.

TECHNIQUES & TACTICS 15

FIRE: Every exceptional effigy employs embers, yet plastered partygoers plus pyre seldomly mix smoothly, so take extra caution. Culinary torches vary greatly in scorching strength, beware before burning.

ICE: To craft large ice molds for punches fill a decorative vessel, such as a bundt cake pan, one-quarter full with non-alcoholic liquid and freeze. Add any fruit or garnishes, and then fill completely with liquid and freeze until solid. To unmold the ice, place the mold into warm water for a few seconds and upturn onto a plate.

DRY ICE: The solid semblance of carbon dioxide, creating clouds of calamity in cocktails. Dangerous to handle without gloves and should never be consumed directly.

GELATIN

**The dark ratio for boozy gelatin is
3 ounces of gelatin powder (flavored or *un*),
8 ounces of boiling non-alcoholic liquid, and
8 ounces of cold or alcoholic liquid.**

Begin by boiling the water or non-alcoholic liquid and pouring it into a heatproof container. Sprinkle the gelatin and stir until completely incorporated. Cool for 20 minutes before adding the alcohol and mixing completely. Pour into individual cups (these recipes make about 16 one ounce shots) or a large decorative mold and refrigerate until completely set: 4 hours for smaller servings and overnight for large molds. When adding ingredients into the gelatin, refrigerate for an hour to firm up before tossing them in. If the gelatin won't release from its decorative dungeon, run the mold under warm water for a few seconds.

SATANIC SYRUPS

THESE STICKY SUSPENSIONS ARE CALLED UPON THROUGHOUT THIS BEDEVILED BOOK TO SHARPEN AND SWEETEN THE ACRID ALCOHOLS WITHIN. WITH RECIPES FOR PLENTIFUL PORTIONS, THERE'S ENOUGH EXCESS TO EXPERIMENT WITH YOUR OWN MALEVOLENT MIXOLOGY.

SIMPLE SYRUP

1 CUP SUGAR
16 OZ. WATER

1. Combine the sugar and water in a small pot on the stovetop and heat on medium until thoroughly mixed.
2. Cool completely before using.

HONEY SYRUP

4 OZ. HONEY
2 OZ. WATER

1. Combine the honey and water in a small pot on the stovetop and heat on medium until thoroughly mixed.
2. Cool completely before using.

VANILLA SYRUP

- WHOLE VANILLA BEAN
- 16 OZ. SUGAR
- 16 OZ. WATER

1. Combine the sugar and water in a small pot on the stovetop and heat on medium until thoroughly mixed.
2. Split the vanilla bean lengthwise and scrape the seeds out with the back of the knife.
3. Add the vanilla seeds and scraped beans and simmer for 5 more minutes.
4. Take syrup off the stovetop and let steep for 45 minutes.
5. Strain and cool completely before using.

JALAPEÑO SYRUP

- 4 TBSP. FRESH JALAPEÑO, FINELY CHOPPED
- 1 CUP SUGAR
- 16 OZ. WATER

1. Combine the sugar and water in a small pot on the stovetop and heat on medium until thoroughly mixed.
2. Add jalapeño and simmer for 5 more minutes.
3. Take syrup off the stovetop and let steep for 45 minutes.
4. Strain and cool completely before using.

SPICED SYRUP

- 1 OZ. CARDAMOM
- 4 WHOLE CINNAMON STICKS
- 16 OZ. SUGAR
- 16 OZ. WATER

1. Combine the sugar and water in a small pot on the stovetop and heat on medium until thoroughly mixed.
2. Add the cinnamon and cardamom and simmer for 5 more minutes.
3. Take syrup off the stovetop and let steep for 45 minutes.
4. Strain and cool completely before using.

GRENADINE

- 16 OZ. SUGAR
- 16 OZ. POMEGRANATE JUICE
- 4 DASHES ORANGE FLOWER WATER

1. Combine the sugar, pomegranate juice, and orange flower water in a small pot on the stovetop and heat on medium until thoroughly mixed.
2. Cool completely before using.

MOCHA SYRUP

- 4 OZ. PREPARED ESPRESSO OR VERY STRONG COFFEE
- 2 OZ. CHOCOLATE SYRUP
- ½ CUP SUGAR

1. Combine the coffee, sugar, and chocolate syrup in a small pot on the stovetop and heat on medium until thoroughly mixed.
2. Cool completely before using.

COLA SYRUP

- 8 OZ. COLA
- 5 DASHES ANGOSTURA BITTERS

1. Combine the cola and bitters in a small pot on the stovetop and heat on medium until thoroughly mixed. Reduce over low heat by ¾.
2. Cool completely before using.

OUR ALL-TIME FAVORITE SERIES!

These little bastards have been slaying away for more than a quarter century, and we've been watching the entire bloody time. Featuring a myriad of murderous marionettes, we've picked a few of our cherished characters to immortalize in cocktail form. Look for the Puppet Master Pick icon and taste all ten in totality!

LET'S PLAY A GAME

If you really wanna tie one on, invite your friends (real or imaginary) to play the Puppet Master Party. Play any movie in the series, prepare a punch bowl of Toulon's Revenge, and one of each of the puppet recipes. Each player picks a puppet and its partnered potable, and must drink when that puppet appears on screen. But beware! When your puppet kills a character, so must you kill your cocktail (it's ok, just assemble an additional recipe or finish the movie out with Toulon). When the tureen of Toulon has been totally tippled, make more puppets and repeat until you run out of movies, mixers, or moxie.

THE PUPPETS

6 Shooter	50	The Tunnler	110
The Blade	71	The Pin Head	113
Miss Leech	73	Torch	114
Toulon's Revenge	89	The Ninja	128
The Jester	91	Decapitron	131

MONSTER SHOTS

These peculiar potables emerge from your nightmares and into your shot glasses. Devilishly designed to look flat-out disgusting, these delicious shooters will scare the shot out of you, until you taste them.

SWAMP JUICE

IT LOOKS LIKE IT CAME STRAIGHT OUT OF THE BLACK LAGOON, BUT THIS STRANGE SHOT WILL HAVE YOU GREEN BEHIND THE GILLS IN NO TIME. IF YOU CAN'T FIND BLACK VODKA, USE PLAIN AND ADD BLACK FOOD COLORING.

½ oz. Green Tea-Infused Black Vodka
½ oz. Chartreuse
½ oz. Lime Juice
Matcha
Sugar

1. Rim a shot glass with the matcha and sugar (see page 15 for rimming instructions).
2. Combine the green tea infused vodka, chartreuse, and lime juice in a cocktail shaker with ice and shake.
3. Strain into the rimmed shot glass.

GREEN TEA-INFUSED BLACK VODKA

750 ml Black Vodka
8 tsp. Green Tea
8 tsp. Sugar

1. Pour yourself a shot or two to make room in the bottle, then throw the tea and sugar into the vodka and let it steep for a day or so—the longer the better.

MONKEY BRAIN

REMEMBER THAT REVOLTING SCENE FROM FACES OF DEATH? THIS ICKY INTOXICANT IS SLIGHTLY LESS GROSS, BUT GUARANTEED TO TASTE TIP-TOP.

- ¾ oz. Peach Brandy
- ¾ oz. Cream Liqueur
- Grenadine (page 18)

1. Pour the peach brandy into a shot glass.
2. Gently pour the cream liqueur over the peach brandy, layering it on top.
3. Wait until the cream liqueur begins to curdle — it'll start looking like a brain.
4. Pour grenadine blood over the top.

FOOL'S GOLD

THERE ONCE WAS A DRUNKARD BY CHANCE

WHEN BOOZED UP HE'D STAMMER AND DANCE

TO HIS FRIENDS HE WOULD TOAST

THEN SLURRINGLY ROAST

AND EVENTUALLY TAKE OFF HIS PANTS

½ oz. Irish Whisky
½ oz. Midori Melon Liqueur
½ oz. Honey Syrup (page 17)

1. Combine the whiskey, Midori, and honey syrup in a cocktail shaker with ice and shake.
2. Strain into a shot glass and drink with a dirty limerick.

BEE'S STING

THIS SWEETLY NAMED SHOT HIDES A CHILI KICK THAT'LL HAVE YOU SCREAMING "CANDY MAN!" FIVE TIMES AFTER YOU DRINK IT.

½ oz. Cinnamon-flavored Whiskey

½ oz. Honey Syrup (page 17)

½ oz. Lemon Juice

Chili Powder

Sugar

1. Rim a shot glass with the chili powder and sugar. See page 15 for rimming instructions.
2. Combine the whiskey, honey syrup, and lemon juice in a cocktail shaker with ice and shake.
3. Strain into the shot glass. Invoke the Candy Man by saying his name five times and watch your party turn to murder.

THE SILVER BULLET

PUT AN END TO THAT BEWHISKERED BEAST INSIDE YOU WITH A FEW OF THESE. TRADE THE TEQUILA WITH GREY GOOSE VODKA FOR AN AMERICAN WEREWOLF IN PARIS.

- 1 can Coors Light
- 2 oz. Silver Tequila

1. Pour the beer into a pint glass.
2. Drop a shot of tequila in. Drink as the bloodlust consumes you—try not to chip your tooth on the shot glass.

DRINK IT WHILE WATCHING *AMERICAN WEREWOLF IN LONDON*

ECTO PLASM

LISTEN, WHEN SOMEONE ASKS YOU IF YOU'RE A SHOT GOD, YOU SAY "YES!"

½ oz. Marshmallow-flavored Vodka

½ oz. Midori Melon Liqueur

½ oz. Mountain Dew

Giant Marshmallow

1. Combine the marshmallow-flavored vodka and Midori in a cocktail shaker with ice and shake.
2. Strain into a shot glass and top with mountain dew.
3. Garnish with a charred giant marshmallow.

DRINK IT WHILE WATCHING

GHOSTBUSTERS

THE SKIN SUIT

IT PUTS THE SHOT IN ITS STOMACH OR ELSE IT GETS THE HOSE AGAIN.

½ oz. Tequila
½ oz. Lime Juice
½ oz. Jalapeño Syrup (page 18)
Chicharrones (Pork Rinds)

1. Combine tequila, lime juice, and jalapeño simple syrup in a cocktail shaker with ice and shake.
2. Strain into a shot glass and garnish with a chicharron.

THE MOTHER HUMPER

BE PREPARED; THIS VULGAR VARIATION OF A CEMENT MIXER WILL HAVE YOUR STOMACH SHUDDERING IF NOT CONSUMED QUICKLY ENOUGH.

- ½ oz. Cream Liqueur
- ½ oz. Lemon Juice
- ½ oz. Simple Syrup (page 18)

1. Pour the cream liqueur into a shot glass
2. Combine the lemon juice and simple syrup into a second shot glass.
3. Drink the shot of lemonade and hold it in your mouth.
4. Drink the shot of cream liqueur and shake your head. Do you feel dumb? You will.

DRINK IT WHILE WATCHING TREMORS

THE 5TH DIMENSION

CROSS OVER INTO INEBRIATION WITH A MONOCHROMATIC MELANGE. THIS VARIATION OF A WHITE RUSSIAN WORKS BEST LAYERED, BUT DON'T DISTRESS IF IT MIXES TOGETHER.

½ oz. Black Vodka
½ oz. Coffee Liqueur
½ oz. Double Cream

1. Combine the vodka and coffee liqueur in a cocktail shaker with ice and shake.
2. Strain into a shot glass and gently pour the cream on top, layering the shot.

DRINK IT WHILE WATCHING THE TWILIGHT ZONE

YOU'RE ICE CREAM!

IN THE MOVIE, THE ICE CREAM MAN'S SICKENING SUNDAES COME COMPLETE WITH EVISCERATED EYEBALLS AND COPS' HEADS. THIS TASTES BETTER.

- ¾ oz. Chocolate Liqueur
- ¾ oz. Walnut Liqueur
- Whipped Cream
- Maraschino Cherry
- Rainbow Sprinkles

1. Combine the chocolate liqueur and walnut liqueur in a cocktail shaker with ice and shake.
2. Strain into a shot glass and garnish with the whipped cream, maraschino cherry, and rainbow sprinkles.

DRINK IT WHILE WATCHING ICE CREAM MAN

MONSTER SMASHED

D.U.H.C.

DRINK UP, HORROR CONNOISSEURS! WITH GLOWING EYES EMERGING FROM MANHOLES, C.H.U.D. TERRORIZED THE STREETS OF NEW YORK CITY. TERRORIZE YOUR BRAIN AND BODY WITH THIS EERILY ENERGIZING COMBINATION OF BOOZE AND COFFEE.

¾ oz. Black Vodka

¾ oz. Coffee Liqueur

Chocolate Sandwich Cookie

Lemon

1. With a paring knife, cut a ½-inch circular medallion from the lemon.

2. Combine the black vodka and coffee liqueur in a cocktail shaker with ice and shake.

3. Strain into a shot glass and drop two small lemon medallions in after expressing the oils.

4. Garnish with the cookie "manhole cover".

HARLEQUIN HOOCH

CLIMB INTO THE COTTON CANDY COCOON AND TAKE OVER THE WORLD WITH THIS SCRUMPTIOUS SHOT.

¾ oz. Cotton Candy-flavored Vodka

¾ oz. White Cranberry Juice

Grenadine (page 18)

Cotton Candy

Maraschino Cherries

1. Stuff a small amount of cotton candy in the bottom of a shot glass and drizzle with the grenadine.
2. Combine the cotton candy-flavored vodka and white cranberry juice in a cocktail shaker with ice and shake.
3. Strain into the shot glass. Garnish with cotton candy hair, a cherry nose, and a crazy straw.

DRINK IT WHILE WATCHING *KILLER KLOWNS FROM OUTER SPACE*

MIDNIGHT MIXERS

TWO DRINKS IN ONE! OUR FAVORITE. GORGE ON THE UNASSUMING MOGWAIS AND YOU'LL TURN INTO A GREMLIN IN NO TIME. JUST MAKE SURE TO EAT YOUR MUNCHIES BEFORE MIDNIGHT.

1 oz. Vodka
1 oz. Cream
1 oz. Simple Syrup (page 17)
Mocha Syrup (page 18)
Mini Marshmallows
Matcha

THE MOGWAI

1. Combine ½ oz. vodka, ½ oz. cream, and ½ oz. simple syrup in a cocktail shaker with ice and shake.
2. Strain into a shot glass and drizzle with mocha syrup.
3. Float mini marshmallows on top and light on fire. Extinguish when charred. Let it cool before drinking the shot!

THE GREMLIN

1. Rim a highball glass with the matcha. (see page 15 for rimming instructions)
2. Combine ½ oz. vodka, ½ oz. cream, ½ oz. simple syrup, and matcha in a cocktail shaker with ice and shake.
3. Strain into the highball glass over ice and dust with matcha.

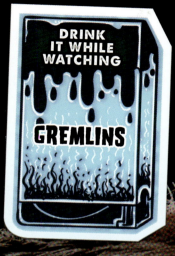

KID COB

YOU MAY FEEL LIKE A CHILD POSSESSED, BUT TRUST US—IF YOU'RE CONTEMPLATING CONSUMING CORN WATER AND MOONSHINE YOUR CHILDHOOD IS FAR, FAR BEHIND YOU.

½ oz. White Whiskey or Moonshine, preferably made from corn
½ oz. Corn Water
½ oz. Lemon Juice
Maraschino Cherry

1. Strain a small can of corn through cheesecloth, separating the water from the kernels and reserving both.
2. Combine the whiskey, ½ oz. corn water, and lemon juice in a cocktail shaker with ice and shake.
3. Strain into a shot glass and garnish with a corn kernel-stuffed maraschino cherry or two.

DRINK IT WHILE WATCHING CHILDREN OF THE CORN

MONSTER SHOTS

6 SHOOTER

WHO WANTS TO PLAY THE ODDS AGAINST THIS SCORCHING SHOT OF PEPPERY PORCINE PALLIATIVE? KEEP A DIE HANDY FOR THIS GAMING DRINK, AND MAYBE A GLASS OF MILK NEARBY TO TEMPER THE TIPPLER'S TONGUE.

2 oz. Bacon-Infused Whiskey

The hottest hot sauce you can find

Candied Bacon

1. Pour the bacon-infused whiskey into a shot glass and garnish with a strip of candied bacon.
2. Roll a die. The number you roll is the number of times 'ol Six Shooter done shot ya. Add one dash of hot sauce for each piece of hot lead.

BACON-INFUSED WHISKEY

½ lb. Smoked Bacon, the smokier the better

12 oz. Whiskey, the better, the better

1. Cook the bacon on a stove top, reserving the rendered fat.
2. Cool the fat enough to safely handle while remaining liquid. Using a funnel, pour carefully into the bottle of whiskey and shake. Eat the bacon.
3. Freeze the bottle of whiskey until the fat solidifies. Strain the fat out completely with cheesecloth (this may take a few passes). Use the whiskey-infused fat for some ridiculous BBQ or something.

CANDIED BACON

½ lb. Thick-sliced Smoked Bacon

¼ cup Light Brown Sugar

Black Pepper

1. In a bowl, season bacon with brown sugar and black pepper.
2. Arrange in a single layer on a parchment-lined baking sheet and bake at 325°F for 20 minutes or until crisp, checking and rotating occasionally.
3. Cool completely before using.

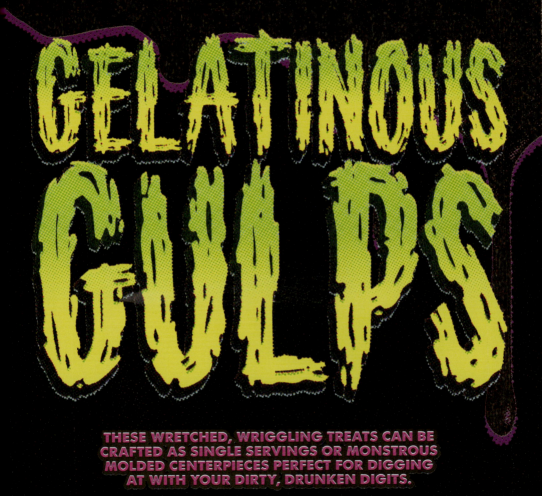

GELATINOUS GULPS

THESE WRETCHED, WRIGGLING TREATS CAN BE CRAFTED AS SINGLE SERVINGS OR MONSTROUS MOLDED CENTERPIECES PERFECT FOR DIGGING AT WITH YOUR DIRTY, DRUNKEN DIGITS.

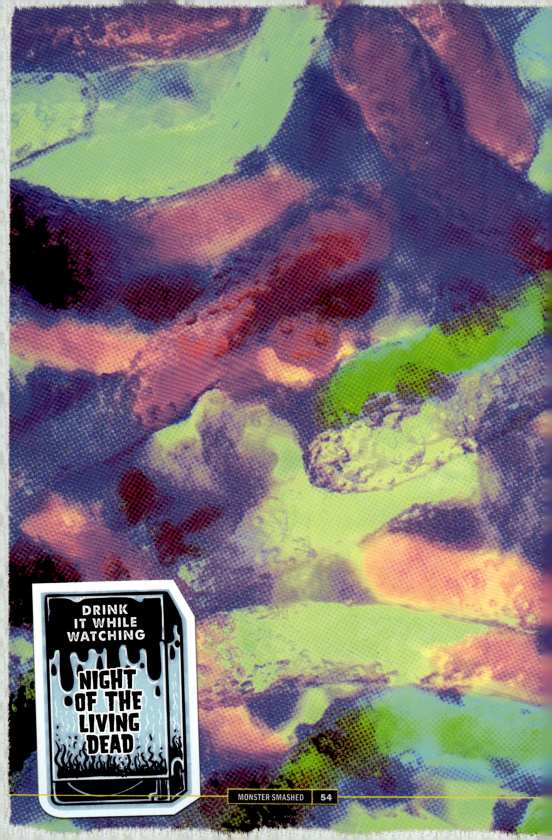

GRAVESITE GROTESQUERY

SERVE THIS BOOZE-FILLED CANDY IN A PILE AND LET YOUR FRIENDS CLAW AT IT LIKE THE BRAINLESS ZOMBIES THEY ARE.

- 8 oz. Vodka
- 6 oz. Fernet Branca
- Gummy Worms
- ½ cup Turbinado Sugar
- 4 oz. Lemon Juice
- 3 oz. Unflavored Gelatin

1. Soak the gummy worms in the vodka in the refrigerator for 12 hours.
2. Combine the lemon juice, 4 oz. water, turbinado sugar, and gelatin in a small pot over low heat and cook until the gelatin dissolves.
3. With the heat off, add the Fernet Branca and mix thoroughly.
4. Refrigerate 10–20 minutes or until slightly set.
5. Toss the worms in the gelatin mixture and arrange in a pile on a wax paper-covered cookie sheet.
6. Chill overnight or until set.
7. Sprinkle with turbinado sugar before eating with your fingers.

CEN-O-BITES

THE LOOK OF THIS CREEPY CENTERPIECE MAY GIVE YOU PINS AND NEEDLES, BUT THE TITILLATING TASTE WILL HAVE YOU RAISING HELL.

- 8 oz. Tequila
- 5 oz. White Cranberry Juice
- 2 oz. Coconut Milk
- 1 oz. Lime Juice
- 3 oz. Unflavored Gelatin
- 2 tbsp. Sugar
- Plastic Face Mask, washed and cleaned
- Toothpicks

1. Combine cranberry juice, coconut milk, lime juice, sugar, and gelatin in a small pot over low heat and cook until the gelatin is dissolved.
2. With the heat off, add the tequila and mix thoroughly.
3. Pour into the face mask and chill overnight or until set.
4. Place a plate over the mask and flip to remove gelatin from the mask.
5. Cut into squares and place toothpicks into each piece.

GELATINOUS GULPS 57

SEWER JELLY

SERVE THIS UP AND WATCH IT TAKE OVER THE PARTY.

- 8 oz. Vodka
- 1 ½ oz. Cherry-flavored Packaged Gelatin
- 1 ½ oz. Grape-flavored Packaged Gelatin
- 8 oz. Vanilla Yogurt
- Pineapple (cut into small chunks)

1. Combine the packaged gelatin and 8 oz. water in a small pot over low heat and cook until the gelatin is dissolved.
2. With the heat off, add the vodka and mix thoroughly.
3. Combine the pineapple chunks with the gelatin and mix.
4. Pour into a bundt cake pan and add the vanilla yogurt. Mix loosely.
5. Chill overnight or until set.

PENNYWISE POTION

I'D TRADE YOU A BALLOON FOR ONE OF THESE ANY DAY, JOHNNY.

- 8 oz. Popcorn Vodka
- 7 oz. Seltzer
- 1 oz. Cola Syrup (page 18)
- 3 oz. Unflavored Gelatin
- Caramel popcorn

1. Combine the seltzer, cola syrup, and gelatin in a small pot over low heat and cook until the gelatin is dissolved.
2. With the heat off, add the popcorn vodka and mix thoroughly.
3. Pour into individual molds or cups.
4. Chill overnight or until set. Garnish with caramel popcorn.

DRINK IT WHILE WATCHING IT

99 MINS

TAKE REVENGE ON YOUR SOBRIETY WITH THIS DECEPTIVELY FIERY SHOT THAT WILL CAUSE YOUR INHIBITIONS TO RAPIDLY DISINTEGRATE AFTER AN HOUR AND A HALF.

- 8 oz. Chocolate liqueur
- 6 ½ oz. Milk
- 1 oz. Chocolate Syrup
- ½ oz. Jalapeño Syrup (page 18)
- 3 oz. Unflavored Gelatin
- Edible Rice paper

1. Combine the milk, chocolate syrup, jalapeño syrup, and gelatin in a small pot over low heat and cook until the gelatin is dissolved.
2. With the heat off, add the chocolate liqueur and mix thoroughly.
3. Pour into individual molds or cups.
4. Chill overnight or until set. Garnish with rice paper "bandages."

BRUNDLEFLY'S RESEARCH

OVERDOSING ON THIS PETRI DISH DELICACY MAY OR MAY NOT GIVE YOU A SUB-HUMAN SEX DRIVE, BUT WILL DEFINITELY MUTATE YOU. BE AFRAID. BE VERY AFRAID.

8 oz. Vodka
8 oz. Lemonade
3 oz. Unflavored Gelatin
Food Coloring
Sprinkles

1. Combine the lemonade and gelatin in a small pot over low heat and cook until the gelatin is dissolved.
2. With the heat off, add the vodka and mix thoroughly.
3. Pour into petri dishes. Refrigerate 10–20 minutes or until slightly set, then decorate with sprinkles and food coloring.
4. Chill overnight or until set.

DRINK IT WHILE WATCHING THE FLY

GELATINOUS GULPS

THE GREEN GHOULIE

YOU'LL EITHER SEE GREEN FACES POPPING *OUT* OF THE TOILET, OR YOUR GREEN FACE WILL BE POPPING *INTO* THE TOILET.

- 4 oz. Applejack
- 4 oz. Licor 43
- 8 oz. Apple Cider
- 3 oz. Unflavored Gelatin
- Green Sourpatch Kids

1. Combine the apple cider and gelatin in a small pot over low heat and cook until the gelatin is dissolved.
2. With the heat off, add the applejack and Licor 43 and mix thoroughly.
3. Pour into individual novelty toilet-bowl-shaped shot glasses.
4. Chill overnight or until set. Garnish with a green Sourpatch Kid.

CHUCKY'S SHOT

HEY, WANNA PLAY?

8 oz. Vodka

¾ oz. Red Packaged Gelatin

¾ oz. Pink Packaged Gelatin

¾ oz. Blue Packaged Gelatin

¾ oz. Light Blue Packaged Gelatin

Grenadine (page 18)

1. Combine the individual packaged gelatin and 2 oz. water each in small pots over low heat and cook until the gelatin is dissolved.

2. With the heat off, add 2 oz. vodka to each pot and mix thoroughly.

3. With a measuring syringe, fill each shot glass with a very small amount of the red gelatin. Chill for 20 minutes or until set.

4. Continue layering the different colors of gelatin, pausing to let each layer set completely before moving on to the next.

5. Once completely set, uncup the shots and serve drizzled with grenadine.

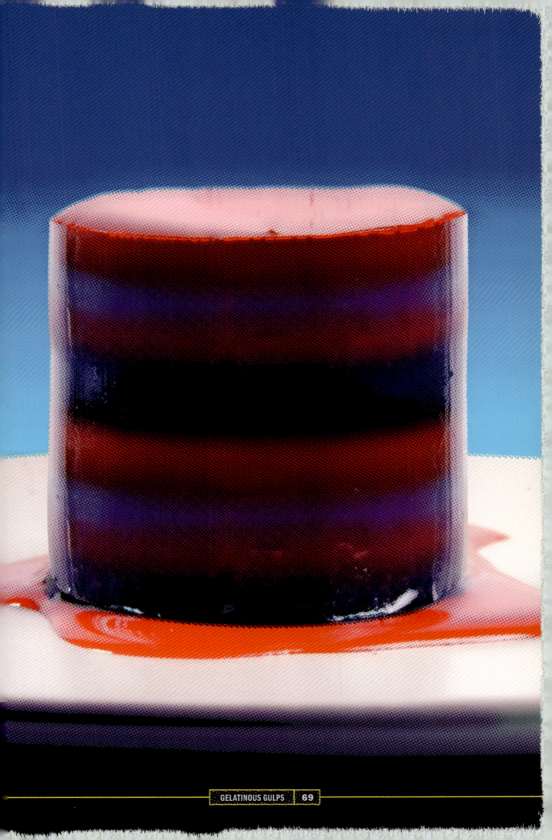

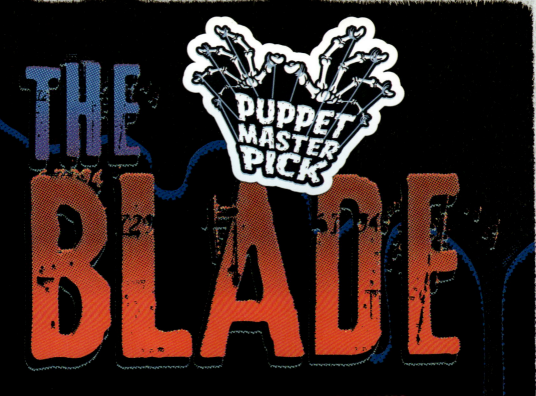

THE BLADE

PUPPET MASTER PICK

THIS HOLLAND RAZOR BLADE VARIATION SLICES AND STABS LIKE A TEENY TINY TERROR.

- 8 oz. Gin
- 4 oz. Lemon Juice
- 4 oz. Simple Syrup (page 17)
- 3 oz. Unflavored Gelatin
- Cayenne Powder

1. Combine the lemon juice, simple syrup, and gelatin in a small pot over low heat and cook until the gelatin is dissolved.
2. With the heat off, add the gin and mix thoroughly.
3. Pour into individual molds or cups.
4. Chill overnight or until set, garnish with cayenne and a novelty razor blade.

DRINK IT WHILE WATCHING **PUPPET MASTER 2**

MISS LEECH

THIS LYCHEE AND ANISE-FLAVORED SHOT HAS A TANTALIZING TWANG. UNLIKE ITS NAMESAKE, TRY NOT TO REGURGITATE IT.

- 6 oz. Black Vodka
- 2 oz. Absinthe
- 3 oz. Lemon Juice
- 3 oz. Simple Syrup (page 17)
- 3 oz. Unflavored Gelatin
- Canned Lychee (2 oz. juice reserved)

1. Combine the lemon juice, simple syrup, lychee juice, and gelatin in a small pot over low heat and cook until the gelatin is dissolved.
2. With the heat off, add the black vodka and absinthe and mix thoroughly.
3. Pour into individual molds or cups.
4. Chill overnight or until set, garnish with a black food coloring-dyed lychee.

POTIONS & GROG

THESE PALATABLE PUNCHES ARE PERFECTLY PORTIONED FOR PLENTIFUL PARTYGOERS (MOST RECIPES MAKE THIRTY 5 OZ. SERVINGS).

Beware the cold-looming spectre of ice—whether as a large decorative piece floating in the bowl or kept on the side in a bucket, as host you must perpetually tread the veil between temperature and dilution. To combat loss of flavor, make the ice using each recipe's non-alcoholic ingredients.

PIRANHA HEAD PUNCH

THERE'S SOMETHING IN THE WATER… WHISKEY.

- 50 oz. Whiskey
- 12 ½ oz. Cognac
- 12 ½ oz. Pear Brandy
- 7 oz. Lemon Juice
- 1 cup Sugar
- Pears
- Lemon Slices
- Cloves

1. Combine the whiskey, cognac, pear brandy, lemon juice, 68 oz. water, and sugar in a punch bowl; mix thoroughly, then chill.
2. Float the fish heads, lemon slices, and ice in the punch.
3. Garnish each cup with a lemon twist.

FISH HEADS

1. Peel the pears and carve into ferocious fish faces using a paring knife.
2. Dehydrate or bake at 150° for 4 hours. Chill until safe to handle.
3. Push cloves into the eye sockets.

DRINK IT WHILE WATCHING
PIRANHA

POTIONS & GROG

CRYPT KEEPER PUNCH

RISING FROM THE DEAD HAS NEVER TASTED SO GOOD. ENJOY THE RIDE, KIDDIES! MUAHAHAHA!

- 30 oz. Gin
- 30 oz. Cointreau
- 30 oz. Lillet blanc
- 10 oz. Absinthe
- 15 oz. Lemon juice
- 5 cups Sugar
- Orange peel

1. Combine the gin, Cointreau, Lillet, absinthe, lemon juice, sugar, and 35 oz. water in a punch bowl and stir until thoroughly mixed.

2. Float orange peels and a large molded ice cube in the punch.

DRINK IT WHILE WATCHING *TALES FROM THE CRYPT*

CAMP CRYSTAL LAKE SANGRIA

THIS LITTLE LETHAL LAKE RUNS RED WITH CAMP COUNSELOR BLOOD, BUT AFTER A SIP YOU MAY FIND YOURSELF NIBBLING ON MORE THAN JUST THE FRUIT.

- 100 oz. Malbec
- 25 oz. Cherry Heering
- 15 oz. Lemon Juice
- 1 cup Sugar
- Cinnamon Sticks
- Cherries
- Blood Oranges
- Grapefruit
- 2 Rubber Gloves

1. Cut cherries in half. Cut oranges and grapefruit into small pieces roughly the same size as the cherry halves.
2. Combine the malbec, cherry heering, lemon juice, 10 oz. water, sugar, and fruit in a punch bowl and mix thoroughly. Let chill and mascerate overnight.
3. Fill two (clean!) rubber gloves with the punch and freeze until solid.
4. Float the ice hands and cinnamon sticks in the punch.

DRINK IT WHILE WATCHING

FRIDAY THE 13TH

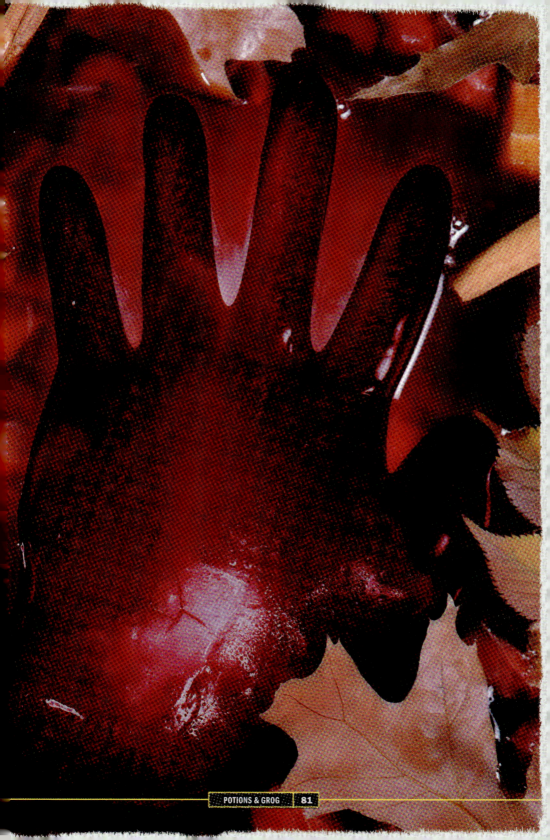

MONSTER SMASHED | 82

BETELGEUSE

NICE FUCKIN MODEL. BRING A LIFELESS PARTY BACK FROM THE DEAD WITH THIS SUPER-SIZED CORPSE REVIVER.

- 50 oz. Whiskey
- 50 oz. Cointreau
- 15 oz. Lillet Blanc
- 15 oz. Lemon Juice
- 20 oz. Orange Juice
- 1 cup Sugar
- Edible Flowers
- Dried Edible Beetle

1. Combine the whiskey, Cointreau, Lillet, lemon juice, orange juice, and sugar in a punch bowl and mix thoroughly.
2. Float the orange peels, flower petals, and a large molded ice cube in the punch.
3. Garnish each glass with a flower and a dried edible beetle.

DRINK IT WHILE WATCHING BEETLEJUICE

PAZUZU'S PUKE

DO YOU WANT TO DRINK DEMONIC PUKE? DO YOUR FRIENDS WANT TO DRINK PUKE? WELL THEN BE OUR GUEST. DRINK PUKE.

- 50 oz. Brandy
- 50 oz. Dark Rum
- 50 oz. Milk (very cold)
- 1 cup Vanilla Sugar
- Green Food Coloring
- Corn Flakes (optional)

1. Combine the brandy, rum, milk, food coloring, and vanilla sugar in a punch bowl and mix thoroughly.
2. If desired, float the corn flakes in the punch.

VANILLA SUGAR

- Vanilla Bean
- 1 cup Sugar

1. Split the vanilla bean lengthwise and combine with the sugar in a glass jar.
2. Let the vanilla bean infuse for at least two weeks, shaking the jar occasionally.
3. Alternatively, cut the bean lengthwise and scrape out the seeds with the back of a knife. Stir into the sugar, making sure to press the seeds with the back of a spoon until thoroughly mixed.
4. Also alternatively, just add ¼ tsp vanilla extract to the sugar.

SOMERSET'S BIG SWIG

COMPLETE JOHN DOE'S MIXOLOGICAL MASTERPIECE AND WATCH THE PARTY GET SPACEY.

- 15 oz. Eagle Rare 10-Year-Old or other American Whiskey (Pride)
- 15 oz. Eagle Rare 17-Year-Old or other 17-Year-Old American Whiskey (Greed)
- 20 oz. Sloe Gin (Sloth)
- 60 oz. Champagne (Gluttony)
- 15 oz. Midori Melon Liqueur (Envy)
- 16 oz. Strawberries (Lust)
- Ghost Pepper (Wrath)

1. Combine the strawberries (reserve a few for garnish) and 2 cups water in a blender and puree until smooth, then strain.
2. Rub the inside of a punch bowl with the ghost chili. Do yourself a favor, wear a disposable glove.
3. Combine the whiskey, gin, midori, and strawberry puree in the punch bowl and mix thoroughly.
4. Float the strawberries and a large molded ice cube in the punch.
5. Top individual cups with champagne.

DRINK IT WHILE WATCHING

SEVEN

TOULON'S REVENGE

THE MAKER'S MASTERFUL MIX. GULP GLASS AFTER GLASS AND HAVE AN OUT-OF-BODY EXPERIENCE. ARE THOSE DOLLS MOVING?

- 60 oz. Vodka
- 40 oz. Midori Melon Liqueur
- 15 oz. Absinthe
- 20 oz. Lemon Juice
- 2 cups Sugar
- Seltzer
- Lime Slices

1. Combine the vodka, midori, absinthe, lemon juice, sugar, and 2 cups water in a punch bowl and mix thoroughly.
2. Float the lime slices and a large molded ice cube in the punch.
3. Top individual cups with seltzer.

DRINK IT WHILE WATCHING PUPPET MASTER 4

THE JESTER

A DARK PUNCH SO PIQUANT IT'LL HAVE YOUR HEAD SPINNING WITH EMOTIONS.

- 60 oz. Dark Rum
- 45 oz. Pineapple Juice
- 45 oz. Blood Orange Juice
- ½ oz. Angostura Bitters
- Lemon Slices
- Lime Slices
- Blood Orange Slices
- Orange Slices

1. Combine the rum, bitters, pineapple juice, and blood orange juice in a punch bowl and mix thoroughly.
2. Float the fruit slices and a large molded ice cube in the punch.
3. Garnish individual cups with citrus slices.

PUPPET MASTER PICK

GECKO BROS. BREW

YOU MAY WANT TO WAIT UNTIL THE SUN GOES DOWN BEFORE FEASTING ON THIS TANGY TEQUILA TIPPLE.

- 50 oz. Tequila
- 25 oz. Mezcal
- 15 oz. Creme de Cassis
- 50 oz. Orange Juice
- 10 oz. Lime Juice
- Seltzer

1. Combine the tequila, mezcal, creme de cassis, orange juice, and lime juice in a punch bowl and mix thoroughly.
2. Float a large molded ice cube in the punch.
3. Top individual cups with seltzer.

BIG FISHBOWL PUNCH

YOU'RE GONNA NEED A BIGGER BELLY.
(MAKES 2 HUGE SERVINGS)

20 oz. White Rum

5 oz. Blue Curaçao

25 oz. Lemon Lime Soda

Shark Gummies

1. Combine the rum, curaçao, and soda in a small fish bowl and mix thoroughly.
2. Float the shark gummies and bloody ice cubes in the punch.

BLOODY ICE CUBES

16 oz. Grenadine (page 18)

16 oz. Frozen Raspberries

1. Combine the grenadine and frozen raspberries with 2 cups water and freeze until solid.

SMOKE & MIRRORS

TOO MUCH TIME ON YOUR HANDS? GO FULL RICK BAKER AND GET CRAFTY CONSTRUCTING THESE TIPPLES WITH A TERRORIFIC TWIST.

BOOM STICK

TURN YOUR FRIENDS INTO AN ARMY OF DARKNESS WITH THIS CRACKLING COCKTAIL.

- 5 oz. Whiskey
- 2 oz. Pineapple Juice
- 1 oz. Lemon Juice
- Pop Rocks Candy

1. Rim a rocks glass with Pop Rocks (see page 15 for rimming instructions).
2. Combine the whiskey, pineapple juice, and lemon juice in a cocktail shaker with ice and shake.
3. Strain into the rocks glass over ice. Garnish with a dual-straw shotgun.

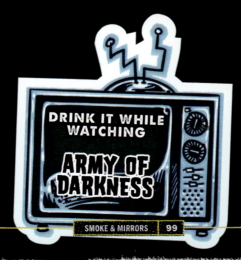

DRINK IT WHILE WATCHING
ARMY OF DARKNESS

TROMAVILLE TIPPLE

YOU MAY BE 98 POUNDS OF SOLID NERD, BUT THIS TOXIC SHOT WILL HAVE YOU FEELING LIKE THE FIRST SUPERHERO FROM NEW JERSEY WITH ITS EERIE BLACK LIGHT-INDUCED GLOW.

- 3 oz. Vodka
- 1 oz. Mezcal
- 2 oz. Energy Drink
- 2 oz. Orange Soda
- Gummy Octopus

1. Combine the vodka, mezcal, and energy drink in a cocktail shaker with ice and shake.
2. Strain into a rocks glass over ice and top with orange soda.
3. Garnish with a gummy octopus mop.

GORILLA WHALE

CRAWL OUT OF THE SEA AND CRUSH SOME BUILDINGS WITH THIS GINZA GULP.

- 3 oz. Bourbon
- 1 oz. Sake
- 1 oz. Lemon Juice
- 1 oz. Orange Juice
- 1 oz. Simple Syrup (page 18)
- 1 oz. Mountain Dew Soda
- Dry Ice

1. Combine the bourbon, lemon juice, and simple syrup in a cocktail shaker with ice and shake.
2. Strain into a highball glass with ice and top with the sake and Mountain Dew.
3. Place the dry ice on the top of the glass. Drink only from the bottom of the glass with a straw.

DRINK IT WHILE WATCHING
GODZILLA VS. MECHAGODZILLA

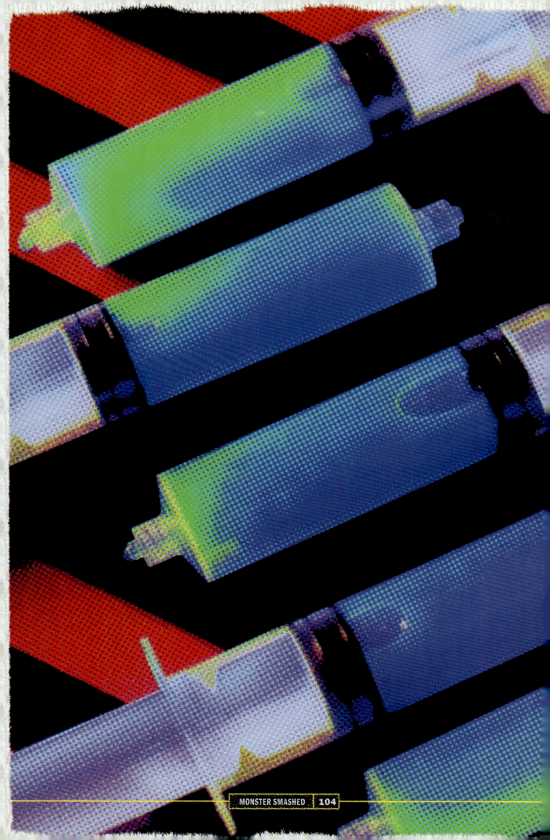

THE DREAM WARRIOR

THIS NEON BLUE SYRINGE SHOT TASTES LIKE A DREAM, BUT A HANDFUL WILL HAVE YOU SEEING NIGHTMARES. (MAKES 10 SINGLE-SERVING SYRINGES)

- 4 oz. Vodka
- 4 oz. Blue Curaçao
- 4 oz. Lemon Juice
- 4 oz. Simple Syrup (page 17)

1. Combine the vodka, Curaçao, lemon juice, and simple syrup in a cocktail shaker with ice and shake.
2. Strain into single-serving-sized syringes.

INJECT IT WHILE WATCHING *NIGHTMARE ON ELM STREET 3*

WATER MELON SKULLS

YOU'D HAVE TO BE BRAIN DEAD TO PASS ON THESE BOOZED-UP CRANIUMS.

- 32 oz. Tequila
- 4 Mini Watermelons
- 8 oz. Lemon juice

1. Cut a hole in each watermelon and pour in 8 oz. of tequila. Chill overnight to macerate.
2. Carve the watermelons into skull shapes. Spritz the exposed flesh with the lemon juice.
3. Use the leftover scraps to make a boozy fruit salad or blend them with a bit more tequila and lemon juice for a daiquiri.

EAT IT WHILE WATCHING

DEAD ALIVE

CLAUDIA

THIS CLASSIC NEW ORLEANS COCKTAIL'S GORGEOUS GOOD LOOKS BETRAY ITS BITE. QUENCH THE FIERY BURN WITH A SWEET, GHOSTLY ICE SPHERE.

- 2 oz. Whiskey
- 2 oz. Cognac
- 2 oz. Sweet Vermouth
- ¼ oz. Benedictine
- 2 dashes Peychaud's Bitters
- 1 dash Angostura Bitters
- Lemon

1. Combine the whiskey, cognac, vermouth, benedictine, and bitters in a cocktail shaker with ice and stir vigorously for 30 seconds.
2. Strain into a rocks glass over a large lemonade ice sphere. Garnish with a lemon twist.

LEMONADE ICE BALL

- 8 oz. Simple Syrup (page 17)
- 8 oz. Lemon Juice

1. Combine ingredients with water and freeze in a novelty sphere-shaped ice cube tray.

DRINK IT WHILE WATCHING *INTERVIEW WITH A VAMPIRE*

THE TUNNELER

GET TUNNEL VISION AND GO DIGGIN'! WHO KNOWS WHAT IT MIGHT BRAINS. WE MEAN, BRING. WHAT IT MIGHT BRING. BRAINS.

- 4 oz. Vodka
- 3 oz. Orange Juice
- 1 oz. Energy Drink

1. Combine the vodka and orange juice in a cocktail shaker with ice and shake.
2. Strain into a highball glass with ice and top with the energy drink.

DRINK IT WHILE WATCHING **PUPPET MASTER 6**

THE PIN HEAD

NO ONE CAN EVER LEGALLY TELL YOU TO DRINK A RAW EGG, SO DON'T. NO ONE'S TELLING YOU TO. EXCEPT FOR COUGHLIN. AND HE'S BEEN DEAD SINCE '88. BLINK, BLINK, BLINKITY, BLINK.

2 oz. Whiskey
7 oz. Lager Beer
1 oz. Tomato Juice
1 Egg
Tabasco

1. Combine the whiskey, tobasco, and tomato juice in a pint glass.
2. Add the beer slowly and then crack the egg into the pint glass.
3. When the egg floats to the top, drink it in one gulp— like a giant man with a tiny head.

DRINK IT WHILE WATCHING
PUPPET MASTER 7

TORCH

ATTEMPT THIS TIPPLE AT THE BEGINNING OF THE PARTY, WHEN YOU'RE SOBER AND PROFESSIONAL.

- 1 oz. 151-Proof Rum
- 1 oz. 99 Bananas
- Marshmallow

1. Light the top of the marshmallow on fire, extinguish after a few seconds. Place burnt marshmallow in a shot glass.
2. Combine the 99 Bananas and rum in a cocktail shaker with ice and shake.
3. Strain into the shot glass over the marshmallow.

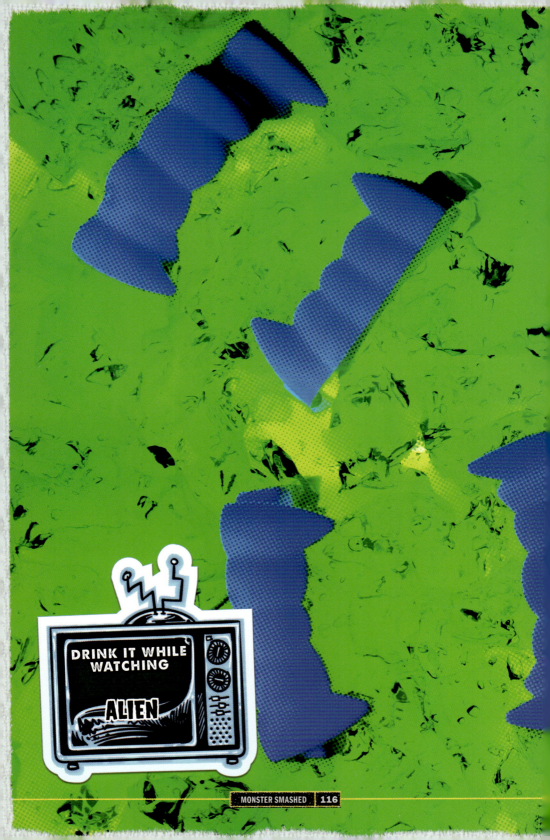

XENOMORPH ENTRAILS

THIS GROSS GOB OF GELATIN GUTS GLOW IN THE PRESENCE OF A BLACKLIGHT, JUST LIKE THE BLOOD OF EVERYONE'S FAVORITE ALIEN.

8 oz. Gin

3 oz. Green Packaged Gelatin

5 oz. Tonic

3 oz. Lime Juice

1. Combine the packaged gelatin, lime juice, and tonic in a small pot over low heat and cook until the gelatin is dissolved.

2. With the heat off, add the gin and mix thoroughly.

3. Chill overnight or until set. Garnish with plastic teeth.

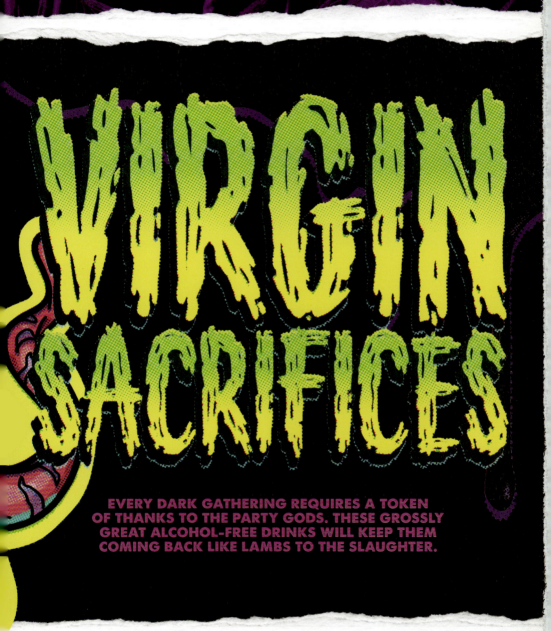

VIRGIN SACRIFICES

EVERY DARK GATHERING REQUIRES A TOKEN OF THANKS TO THE PARTY GODS. THESE GROSSLY GREAT ALCOHOL-FREE DRINKS WILL KEEP THEM COMING BACK LIKE LAMBS TO THE SLAUGHTER.

TAD'S TANGY TUMBLER

THIS PUCKERING POTABLE WILL HAVE THE MOST TIMID PUP FOAMING AT THE MOUTH. IF YOU CRAVE JUST A LITTLE HAIR OF THE DOG, TRY ADDING TEQUILA OR MEZCAL.

- 4 oz. Grapefruit Juice
- 4 oz. Lemon-lime Soda
- 2 oz. Pomegranate Juice
- 2 grams Soy Lecithin
- Salt

1. Combine the pomegranate juice, salt, and soy lecithin in a bowl. Aerate with a hand blender for 3 minutes, or until it foams up.
2. Combine the grapefruit juice and lemon-lime soda in a rocks glass with ice and stir.
3. Spoon the foam on top and garnish with a straw.

VIRGIN SACRIFICES

BROOMSTICK PUNCH

EVEN IF YOU'RE THE DESIGNATED DRIVER, YOU'LL STILL FEEL LIKE YOU'VE BEEN RUNNING THROUGH THE WOODS ALL NIGHT. REPLACE THE SPARKLING JUICE WITH CHAMPAGNE FOR THAT SHAKY-CAM EFFECT. (*MAKES THIRTY 5 OZ. SERVINGS*)

85 oz. Sparkling Grape Juice

35 oz. Concord Grape Juice

15 oz. Lemon Juice

15 oz. Spiced Syrup (page 18)

Cinnamon Sticks

1. Combine the sparkling grape juice, concord grape juice, lemon juice, and spiced syrup in a punch bowl and mix thoroughly.

2. Float the cinnamon sticks and a large molded ice cube in the punch.

DRINK IT WHILE WATCHING THE BLAIR WITCH PROJECT

THE LAWN MOWER

A FEW OF THESE AND YOU'LL BE DOING LAPS AROUND THE FRONT YARD. ADD A COUPLE SPLASHES OF GIN OR VODKA TO TAP INTO A DIFFERENT REALITY.

- 1 oz. Wheat Grass Juice
- 1 oz. Spinach Juice
- 2 oz. Lemon Juice
- 4 oz. Seltzer
- Cucumber
- Lemon

1. Combine the wheat grass, spinach juice, and lemon juice in a cocktail shaker with ice and shake.
2. Strain into a highball glass with ice and top with seltzer.
3. Garnish with a cucumber spear and a lemon wedge.

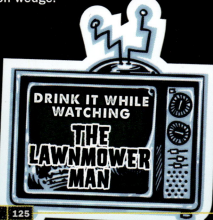

DRINK IT WHILE WATCHING THE LAWNMOWER MAN

CRIMSON WAVE

THIS VIRGIN BLOODY MARY IS SURE TO DELIGHT, BUT THEN YOU'LL GET DRENCHED IN PIG'S BLOOD. THEN YOU'LL GET YOUR PERIOD. SET THE ROOM ON FIRE BY ADDING VODKA.

- 7 oz. Tomato Juice
- 1 oz. Lemon Juice
- 2 Dashes Worcestershire Sauce
- Celery Salt
- Pepper
- Hot Sauce
- Pickled Red Carrot

1. Combine everything but the carrot in a cocktail shaker with ice and shake.
2. Strain into a highball glass with ice.
3. Garnish with a pickled red carrot. Drink half and spill the rest on yourself.

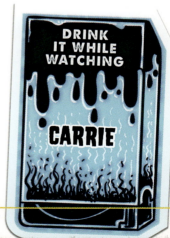

DRINK IT WHILE WATCHING CARRIE

THE NINJA

THIS SPICY TAKE ON A CLASSIC WILL RESULT IN GLOWING RED EYES IN NO TIME. ADD WHISKEY TO GIVE THIS SOFT DRINK THE SHURIKEN'S SPIKE.

- 3 ½ oz. Cola
- 1 oz. Grenadine (page 18)
- ½ oz. Spiced Syrup (page 18)
- 2 dashes Angostura Bitters
- Red Hots

1. Combine the cola, grenadine, spiced syrup, and bitters in a rocks glass with ice and stir.
2. Garnish with Red Hots.

PUPPET MASTER PICK

DECAPITRON

FOLLOWING THE LEADER OF THE PUPPETS WITH THIS FIERY FLAGON MAY RESULT IN IMMOLATION, BUT THAT'S OK, YOU CAN ALWAYS GET ANOTHER HEAD. THROW SOME CINNAMON WHISKEY IN IF THE SPICE LEVEL ISN'T UP TO SNUFF.

- 8 oz. Milk
- 2 oz. Dark Chocolate
- Whipped Cream
- Cinnamon
- Cardamom
- Cayenne
- Salt

1. Combine the milk and chocolate in a small pot on the stovetop and heat on medium until thoroughly mixed.
2. Add the cinnamon, cardamom, cayenne, and salt and simmer for 5 more minutes.
3. Strain into a mug and garnish with whipped cream and a dusting of cinnamon.

BBBRRRAAAIIINNNSSSS!!!

YOU DON'T HAVE TO BE A ZOMBIE PUNK TO ENJOY THIS BRIGHT PINK HORDE-PLEASER, BUT AFTER ONE SIP YOU'LL DEFINITELY BE CRAVING MORE. JUST LIKE THE UNDEAD, THIS DRINK DOESN'T DISCRIMINATE—ADD JUST ABOUT ANY ALCOHOL TO THIS ONE TO KEEP YOU ABOVE THE GRAVE.

2 oz. Lemon juice
1 oz. Simple Syrup (page 17)
1 oz. Grenadine (page 18)
Frozen Raspberries

1. Combine the lemon juice, simple syrup, grenadine, and 4 oz. water in a cocktail shaker with ice and shake.
2. Strain into a rocks glass with ice and garnish with frozen raspberries.

DRINK IT WHILE WATCHING

RETURN OF THE LIVING DEAD 3

MANON

A PROTOTYPICAL POTABLE GOTHED OUT JUST IN TIME FOR THE '90s. WICKED WITCHES CAN ADD GIN TO TRANSFORM THEIR BEVERAGE INTO A BOOZER. THIS IS THE WEIRD DRINK, MISTER.

- 7 oz. Lemon Lime Soda
- 1 oz. Grenadine (page 18)
- Black Gel Food Coloring
- Cherries
- Sugar
- Chili powder

1. Rim a rocks glass with the chili powder and sugar. (see page 15 for rimming instructions)
2. Combine the soda, grenadine, and food coloring in the rocks glass with ice and stir.
3. Garnish with cherries.

DRINK IT WHILE WATCHING THE CRAFT

PUMPKINHEAD

CONJURE THE DEMON OF REVENGE AND GORGE ON THIS GOURD-FLAVORED GOBLET. SILENCE THIS SUPERSTITION WITH VODKA IF IT'S VITAL.

7 oz. Ginger Beer
1 oz. Lemon Juice
1 oz. Pureed Pumpkin
2 oz. Milk
Pumpkin Spice

1. Combine the milk and ¾ oz. of the pureed pumpkin in a bowl. Aerate with a hand blender for 3 minutes, or until it foams up.
2. Combine the ginger beer, remaining pumpkin puree, and lemon juice in a highball glass with ice and stir.
3. Top with the foam and dust with the pumpkin spice.

PUMPKIN SPICE

3 tbsp Ground Cinnamon
2 tsp Ground Ginger
2 tsp Ground Nutmeg
1 tsp Ground Allspice
1 tsp Ground Cloves

1. Combine everything in a small bowl and mix thoroughly.

DRINK IT WHILE WATCHING
PUMPKIN HEAD

THE DEWEY FIZZ

THIS VIRGIN VARIATION OF THE CLASSIC FIZZ WILL HAVE YOUR GUESTS SCREAMING SUCH BLOODY MURDER IT MIGHT MAKE THE NEWS. ADD SOME GIN FOR THAT TIMELESS THIRD-ACT PLOT TWIST.

- 2 oz. Coconut Water
- 1 oz. Pineapple Juice
- 1 oz. Heavy Cream
- 1 oz. Lime Juice
- 1 oz. Vanilla Syrup (page 18)
- 4 dashes Orange Flower Water
- Egg White
- 2 oz. Club soda
- Black Gel Food Coloring

1. Combine the coconut water, pineapple juice, heavy cream, lime juice, vanilla syrup, and orange flower water in a cocktail shaker with ice and shake vigorously for an extended time, until everything is nice and foamy.

2. Strain into a highball glass decorated with food coloring, top with club soda.

DRINK IT WHILE WATCHING

SCREAM

INDEX

NOTE: PAGE NUMBERS IN *ITALICS* INDICATE DRINK RECIPES.

A

Absinthe
  about, 10
  Crypt Keeper Punch, *79*
  Miss Leech, *73*
  Toulon's Revenge, *89*
Angostura Bitters, about, 11
Applejack
  about, 9
  The Green Ghoulie, *67*

B

Bacon-infused Whiskey, in 6 Shooter, *50–51*
Bbbrrraaaiiinnsss!!!, *133*
Beer
  about, 10
  The Pin Head, *113*
  The Silver Bullet, *31*
Bee's Sting, *28–29*
Bénédictine
  about, 10
  Claudia, *109*
Betelgeuse, *83*
Big Fishbowl Punch, *94–95*
Black Vodka. *See* Vodka
Blacklight, 14
Blade, The, *71*
Blenders, 13
Blue Curacao
  about, 11
  Big Fishbowl Punch, *94–95*
  The Dream Warrior, *105*
Boom Stick, *99*

Bourbon, in Gorilla Whale, *102–103*
Brandy. *See also* Applejack
  about, 9
  Monkey Brain, *25*
  Pazuzu's Puke, *85*
  Piranha Head Punch, *77*
Broomstick Punch, *122–123*
Brundlefly's Research, *65*
Bundt cake pan, 13

C

Cen-o-Bites, *56–57*
Champagne
  about, 10
  Somerset's Big Swig, *86–87*
Chartreuse
  about, 10
  Swamp Juice, *23*
Cheesecloth, 14
Cherry Heering
  about, 10
  Camp Crystal Lake Sangria, *80–81*
Chocolate Liqueur
  about, 11
  99 Mins, *62–63*
  You're Ice Cream!, *40–41*
Chucky's Shot, *68–69*
Cinnamon-flavored Whiskey, in Bee's Sting, *28–29*

Claudia, *109*
Cocktail shaker, 13
Cocktail strainer, 13
Coffee Liqueur
  about, 11
  D.U.H.C., *43*
  The 5th Dimension, *39*
Cognac
  about, 9
  Claudia, *109*
  Piranha Head Punch, *77*
Cointreau
  about, 10
  Betelgeuse, *83*
  Crypt Keeper Punch, *79*
Cola Syrup, 18
Cookie sheets, 13
Cotton Candy-flavored Vodka, in Harlequin Hooch, *45*
Cream Liqueur
  about, 11
  Monkey Brain, *25*
  The Mother Humper, *36–37*
Creme de Cassis
  about, 11
  Gecko Bros. Brew, *93*
Crimson Wave, *127*
Crypt Keeper Punch, *79*
Culinary torch, 14, 16

D

Decapitron, *131*
Dewey Fizz, The, *139*
Dream Warrior, The, *105*
Dry ice, 16
D.U.H.C., *43*

MONSTER SMASHED | 140

E
Ecto Plasm, *33*
Energy drinks, about, *11*

F
Fernet-Branca
 about, *10*
 Gravesite Grotesquery, *55*
5th Dimension, The, *39*
Fire, torches and, *14*, *16*
Flavor infusions. *See* Infusions
Fool's Gold, *27*

G
Gecko Bros. Brew, *93*
Gelatinous Gulps, *53–73*
 about: Gelatin recipe for, *16*; overview of, *53*
 The Blade, *71*
 Brundlefly's Research, *65*
 Cen-o-Bites, *56–57*
 Chucky's Shot, *68–69*
 Gravesite Grotesquery, *55*
 The Green Ghoulie, *67*
 Miss Leech, *73*
 99 Mins, *62–63*
 Pennywise Potion, *61*
 Sewer Jelly, *59*
Gin
 about, *9*
 The Blade, *71*
 Crypt Keeper Punch, *79*
 Somerset's Big Swig, *86–87*
 Xenomorph Entrails, *117*
Ginger beer, about, *10*
Glassware
 rimming, *15*
 types of, *14*
Gloves, rubber, *14*
Gorilla Whale, *102–103*
Gravesite Grotesquery, *55*
Green Ghoulie, The, *67*
Green Tea-Infused Black Vodka, *23*
Grenadine, *18*

H
Harlequin Hooch, *45*
Highball glass, *14*
Honey Syrup, *17*

I
Ice, dry, *16*
Ice ball, lemonade, *109*
Ice cubes, bloody, *94*
Ice molds, *16*
Infusions
 about: creating, *15*
 Bacon-infused Whiskey, *50–51*
 Green Tea-Infused Black Vodka, *23*
Ingredients, *8–11*. *See also specific spirits/ alcohol ingredients*

J
Jalapeño Syrup, *18*
Jell-O™ shots. *See* Gelatinous Gulps
Jester, The, *91*
Jigger, about, *13*
Juices, about, *11*

K
Kid Cob, *49*
Knives, *13*

L
Lawnmower, The, *125*
Layering drinks, *15*
Lemonade Ice Ball, *109*
Licor 43 (Cuarenta y tres)
 about, *10*
 The Green Ghoulie, *67*
Lillet Blanc
 about, *10*
 Betelgeuse, *83*
 Crypt Keeper Punch, *79*

M
Malbec
 about, *10*
 Camp Crystal Lake Sangria, *80–81*
Manon, *134–135*
Marshmallow-flavored Vodka, in Ecto Plasm, *33*
Mask, plastic, *14*
Mason jar, *14*
Matcha, about, *11*
Measuring cups, *13*
Mezcal
 about, *9*
 Gecko Bros. Brew, *93*
 Tromaville Tipple, *101*
Midnight Mixers, *46–47*
Midori Melon Liqueur
 about, *11*
 Ecto Plasm, *33*
 Fool's Gold, *27*
 Somerset's Big Swig, *86–87*
 Toulon's Revenge, *89*
Miss Leech, *73*
Mixing glass, *13*
Mocha Syrup, *18*
Monkey Brain, *25*
Monster Shots, *21–51*
 about: overview of, *21*
 Bee's Sting, *28–29*
 D.U.H.C., *43*
 Ecto Plasm, *33*
 The 5th Dimension, *39*
 Fool's Gold, *27*
 Harlequin Hooch, *45*
 Kid Cob, *49*
 Midnight Mixers, *46–47*
 Monkey Brain, *25*
 The Mother Humper, *36–37*
 The Silver Bullet, *31*
 6 Shooter, *50–51*
 The Skin Suit, *35*
 Swamp Juice, *23*
 You're Ice Cream!, *40–41*
Moonshine, in Kid Cob, *49*

Mother Humper,
The, *36–37*
Movies to watch
while drinking
Alien, 116
*American Werewolf
in London,* 31
Army of Darkness, 99
Beetlejuice, 83
*The Blair Witch
Project,* 122
The Blob, 58
Candy Man, 29
Carrie, 127
Children of the Corn, 49
Child's Play?, 68
C.H.U.D., 43
The Craft, 134
*Creature from the
Black Lagoon,* 22
Cujo, 120
Darkman, 63
Dead Alive, 107
From Dusk Till Dawn, 92
The Exorcist, 85
Faces of Death, 25
The Fly, 65
Friday the 13th, 80
Ghostbusters, 33
Ghoulies, 66
*Godzilla VS
Mechagodzilla,* 102
Gremlins, 47
Hellraiser, 57
Ice Cream Man, 40
*Interview with a
Vampire,* 109
It, 61
Jaws, 95
*Killer Klowns from Outer
Space,* 45
*The Lawnmower
Man,* 125
Leprechaun, 26
Night of the Living Dead,
54
*Nightmare on Elm Street
3,* 105
Piranha, 77
Pumpkin Head, 137
Puppet Master, 51
Puppet Master 10, 130
Puppet Master 2, 71
Puppet Master 3, 72
Puppet Master 4, 89
Puppet Master 5, 90
Puppet Master 6, 110
Puppet Master 7, 113
Puppet Master 8, 114
Puppet Master 9, 129
*Return of the Living
Dead 3,* 133
Seven, 86
*Silence of the
Lambs,* 34
Tales from the Crypt, 79
The Toxic Avenger, 101
Tremors, 36
The Twilight Zone, 39

N

99 Bananas
about, 11
Torch, *114–115*
99 Mins, *62–63*
Ninja, The, *128–129*
Non-alcoholic drinks.
See Virgin Sacrifices
(non-alcoholic)

O

Orange flower
water, about, 11

P

Pazuzu's Puke, *85*
Peach Brandy, in
Monkey Brain, *25*
Pear Brandy, in Piranha
Head Punch, *77*
Pennywise Potion, *61*
Petri dishes, 13
Peychaud's Bitters,
about, 11
Pin Head, The, *113*
Pint glass, 14
Piranha Head Punch, *77*
Popcorn Vodka, in
Pennywise Potion, *61*
Pot, cooking, 14
Potions and Grog
(punches), *75–95*

about: ice molds
for punches, 16;
making, 75
Betelgeuse, *83*
Big Fishbowl
Punch, *94–95*
Bloody Ice Cubes, *94*
Broomstick Punch
(non-alcoholic),
122–123
Camp Crystal Lake
Sangria, *80–81*
Crypt Keeper Punch, *79*
Gecko Bros. Brew, *93*
The Jester, *91*
Pazuzu's Puke, *85*
Piranha Head
Punch, *77*
Somerset's Big
Swig, *86–87*
Toulon's Revenge, *89*
Pumpkin Spice, *137*
Pumpkinhead, *137*
Punch glass, 14
Punches. See
Potions and Grog
Puppet Master
Party, 19
Puppet Master Picks
The Blade, *71*
Decapitron, *131*
The Jester, *91*
Miss Leech, *73*
The Ninja, *128–129*
The Pin Head, *113*
6 Shooter, *50–51*
Torch, *114–115*
Toulon's Revenge, *89*
The Tunneler, *110*

R

Rimming glasses, 15
Rocks glass, 14
Rum
about, 9
Big Fishbowl
Punch, *94–95*
The Jester, *91*
Pazuzu's Puke, *85*
Torch, *114–115*

S

Sake
  about, 10
  Gorilla Whale, *102–103*
Sewer Jelly, *59*
Shaker, cocktail, 13
Shaking, straining drinks, 15
Shot glass, 14
Shots. *See* Gelatinous Gulps; Monster Shots
Silver Bullet, The, *31*
Simple Syrup, 17
6 Shooter, *50–51*
Skin Suit, The, *35*
Smoke & Mirrors, *97–117*
  Boom Stick, *99*
  Claudia, *109*
  The Dream Warrior, *105*
  Gorilla Whale, *102–103*
  The Pin Head, *113*
  Torch, *114–115*
  Tromaville Tipple, *101*
  The Tunneler, *110–111*
  Watermelon Skulls, *107*
  Xenomorph Entrails, *117*
Somerset's Big Swig, *86–87*
Soy lecithin, about, 11
Spiced Syrup, *18*
Spirits and ingredients, about, 8–11. *See also specific spirits/ alcohol ingredients*
Spoon, stirring, 13
Stirring spoon, 13
Strainer, cocktail, 13
Straining drinks, 15
Sugar, vanilla, *85*
Swamp Juice, *23*
Syringes, 13
Syrups, *17–18*

T

Tad's Tangy Tumbler, *121*
Techniques and tactics, 15–16
Tequila
  about, 9
  Cen-o-Bites, *56–57*
  Gecko Bros. Brew, *93*
  The Silver Bullet, *31*
  The Skin Suit, *35*
  Watermelon Skulls, *107*
Tipples. *See* Smoke & Mirrors
Tools of the trade, 12–14
Torch, *114–115*
Torch, culinary, 14, 16
Toulon's Revenge, *89*
Tromaville Tipple, *101*
Tunneler, The, *110–111*

V

Vanilla Sugar, *85*
Vanilla Syrup, *18*
Vermouth (sweet), in Claudia, *109*
Virgin Sacrifices (non-alcoholic), *119–139*
  Bbbrrraaaiiinnsss!!!, *133*
  Broomstick Punch, *122–123*
  Crimson Wave, *127*
  Decapitron, *131*
  The Dewey Fizz, *139*
  The Lawnmower, *125*
  Manon, *134–135*
  The Ninja, *128–129*
  Pumpkinhead, *137*
  Tad's Tangy Tumbler, *121*
Vodka
  about, 9
  Brundlefly's Research, *65*
  Chucky's Shot, *68–69*
  The Dream Warrior, *105*
  D.U.H.C., *43*
  Ecto Plasm, *33*
  The 5th Dimension, *39*
  Gravesite Grotesquery, *55*
  Green Tea-Infused Black Vodka, *23*
  Harlequin Hooch, *45*
  Midnight Mixers, *46–47*
  Miss Leech, *73*
  Pennywise Potion, *61*
  Sewer Jelly, *59*
  Swamp Juice, *23*
  Toulon's Revenge, *89*
  Tromaville Tipple, *101*
  The Tunneler, *110–111*

W

Walnut Liqueur
  about, 10
  You're Ice Cream!, *40–41*
Watermelon Skulls, *107*
Wax paper, 14
Whiskey
  about, 9
  Bacon-infused Whiskey, *50–51*
  Bee's Sting, *28–29*
  Betelgeuse, *83*
  Boom Stick, *99*
  Claudia, *109*
  Fool's Gold, *27*
  Gorilla Whale, *102–103*
  Kid Cob, *49*
  The Pin Head, *113*
  Piranha Head Punch, *77*
  6 Shooter, *50–51*
  Somerset's Big Swig, *86–87*
Wine. *See* Champagne; Malbec

X

Xenomorph Entrails, *117*

Y

You're Ice Cream!, *40–41*

Copyright © 2017 by Jon Chaiet & Marc Chaiet

Library of Congress Control Number: 2017933340

All rights reserved. No part of this work may be reproduced or used in any form or by any means—graphic, electronic, or mechanical, including photocopying or information storage and retrieval systems—without written permission from the publisher.

The scanning, uploading, and distribution of this book or any part thereof via the Internet or any other means without the permission of the publisher is illegal and punishable by law. Please purchase only authorized editions and do not participate in or encourage the electronic piracy of copyrighted materials.

"Schiffer," "Schiffer Publishing, Ltd.," and the pen and inkwell logo are registered trademarks of Schiffer Publishing, Ltd.

Photography: Irinia Anisimova

Book design by Chaiet Studios
Typeset in ITC Franklin Gothic, A Love of Thunder, Dirty House, House of Horror, House of Terror, & Urban Decay.

ISBN: 978-0-7643-5370-3
Printed in China

Published by Schiffer Publishing, Ltd.
4880 Lower Valley Road
Atglen, PA 19310
Phone: (610) 593-1777; Fax: (610) 593-2002
E-mail: Info@schifferbooks.com
Web: www.schifferbooks.com

For our complete selection of fine books on this and related subjects, please visit our website at www.schifferbooks.com. You may also write for a free catalog.

Schiffer Publishing's titles are available at special discounts for bulk purchases for sales promotions or premiums. Special editions, including personalized covers, corporate imprints, and excerpts, can be created in large quantities for special needs. For more information, contact the publisher.

We are always looking for people to write books on new and related subjects. If you have an idea for a book, please contact us at proposals@schifferbooks.com.